A

C

Discover

and eas

Table of Content

Adobo Seasoned Chicken with Veggies

(Ready in about 1 hour 30 minutes | Servings 4)

Per serving:

427 Calories; 15.3g Fat; 18.5g Carbs; 52.3g Protein; 9.4g Sugars

Ingredients

2 pounds chicken wings, rinsed and patted dry 1 teaspoon coarse sea salt

1/4 teaspoon ground black pepper

1/2 teaspoon red pepper flakes, crushed 1 teaspoon ground cumin

1 teaspoon paprika

1 teaspoon granulated onion 1 teaspoon ground turmeric 2 tablespoons tomato powder

1 tablespoon dry Madeira wine 2 stalks celery, diced

2 cloves garlic, peeled but not chopped

1 large Spanish onion, diced

2 bell peppers, seeded and sliced 4 carrots, trimmed and halved

2 tablespoons olive oil

Directions

Toss all ingredients in a large bowl. Cover and let it sit for 1 hour in your refrigerator.

Add the chicken wings to a baking pan.

Roast the chicken wings in the preheated Air Fryer at 380 degrees F for 7 minutes.

Add the vegetables and cook an additional 15 minutes, shaking the basket once or twice. Serve warm.

Agave Mustard Glazed Chicken

(Ready in about 30 minutes | Servings 4)

Per serving:

471 Calories; 24.6g Fat; 13.1g Carbs; 47.4g Protein; 12.7g Sugars

Ingredients

1 tablespoon avocado oil

2 pounds chicken breasts, boneless, skin-on 1 tablespoon Jamaican Jerk Rub

1/2 teaspoon salt

3 tablespoons agave syrup 1 tablespoon mustard

2 tablespoons scallions, chopped

Directions

Start by preheating your Air Fryer to 370 degrees F.

Drizzle the avocado oil all over the chicken breast. Then, rub the chicken breast with the Jamaican Jerk rub.

Cook in the preheated Air Fryer approximately 15 minutes. Turn them over and cook an additional 8 minutes.

While the chicken breasts are roasting, combine the salt, agave syrup, and mustard in a pan over medium heat. Let it simmer until the glaze thickens.

After that, brush the glaze all over the chicken breast. Air-fry for a further 6 minutes or until the surface is crispy. Serve garnished with fresh scallions.

Bon appétit!

Asian Chicken Filets with Cheese

(Ready in about 50 minutes | Servings 2)

Per serving:

376 Calories; 19.6g Fat; 12.1g Carbs; 36.2g Protein; 3.4g Sugars

Ingredients

4 rashers smoked bacon 2 chicken filets

1/2 teaspoon coarse sea salt

1/4 teaspoon black pepper, preferably freshly ground 1 teaspoon garlic, minced

1 (2-inch) piece ginger, peeled and minced

1 teaspoon black mustard seeds 1 teaspoon mild curry powder 1/2 cup coconut milk

1/3 cup tortilla chips, crushed

1/2 cup Pecorino Romano cheese, freshly grated

Directions

Start by preheating your Air Fryer to 400 degrees F.

Add the smoked bacon and cook in the preheated Air Fryer for 5 to 7 minutes. Reserve.

In a mixing bowl, place the chicken fillets, salt, black pepper, garlic, ginger, mustard seeds, curry powder, and milk. Let it marinate in your refrigerator about 30 minutes.

 In another bowl, mix the crushed chips and grated Pecorino Romano cheese.

Dredge the chicken fillets through the chips mixture and transfer them to the cooking basket. Reduce the temperature to 380 degrees F and cook the chicken for 6 minutes.

Turn them over and cook for a further 6 minutes. Repeat the process until you have run out of ingredients.

Serve with reserved bacon. Enjoy!

Chicken Sausage Frittata with Cheese

(Ready in about 15 minutes | Servings 2)

Per serving:

475 Calories; 34.2g Fat; 5.3g Carbs; 36.2g Protein; 2.6g Sugars

Ingredients

1 tablespoon olive oil

2 chicken sausages, sliced 4 eggs

1 garlic clove, minced

1/2 yellow onion, chopped

Sea salt and ground black pepper, to taste 4 tablespoons Monterey-Jack cheese

1 tablespoon fresh parsley leaves, chopped

Directions

Grease the sides and bottom of a baking pan with olive oil.

Add the sausages and cook in the preheated Air Fryer at 360 degrees F for 4 to 5 minutes.

In a mixing dish, whisk the eggs with garlic and onion. Season with salt and black pepper.

Pour the mixture over sausages. Top with cheese. Cook in the preheated Air Fryer at 360 degrees F for another 6 minutes.

Serve immediately with fresh parsley leaves. Bon appétit!

Chicken with Golden

(Ready in about 30 minutes | Servings 4)

Per serving:

388 Calories; 18.9g Fat; 5.6g Carbs; 47.3g Protein; 1.3g Sugars

Ingredients

2 pounds chicken legs 2 tablespoons olive oil 1 teaspoon sea salt

1/2 teaspoon ground black pepper 1 teaspoon smoked paprika

1 teaspoon dried marjoram

1 (1-pound) head cauliflower, broken into small florets 2 garlic cloves, minced

1/3 cup Pecorino Romano cheese, freshly grated

1/2 teaspoon dried thyme Salt, to taste

Directions

Toss the chicken legs with the olive oil, salt, black pepper, paprika, and marjoram.

Cook in the preheated Air Fryer at 380 degrees F for 11 minutes. Flip the chicken legs and cook for a further 5 minutes.

Toss the cauliflower florets with garlic, cheese, thyme, and salt.

Increase the temperature to 400 degrees F; add the cauliflower florets and cook for 12 more minutes. Serve warm.

Chinese Duck (Xiang Su Ya)

(Ready in about 30 minutes + marinating time | Servings 6)

Per serving:

403 Calories; 25.3g Fat; 16.4g Carbs; 27.5g Protein; 13.2g Sugars

Ingredients

2 pounds duck breast, boneless 2 green onions, chopped

1 tablespoon light soy sauce

1 teaspoon Chinese 5-spice powder 1 teaspoon Szechuan peppercorns 3 tablespoons Shaoxing rice wine 1 teaspoon coarse salt

1/2 teaspoon ground black pepper Glaze:

1/4 cup molasses

3 tablespoons orange juice 1 tablespoon soy sauce

Directions

In a ceramic bowl, place the duck breasts, green onions, light soy sauce, Chinese 5-spice powder, Szechuan peppercorns, and Shaoxing rice wine. Let it marinate for 1 hour in your refrigerator.

Preheat your Air Fryer to 400 degrees F for 5 minutes.

Now, discard the marinade and season the duck breasts with salt and pepper. Cook the duck breasts for 12 to 15 minutes or until they are golden brown.

Repeat with the other ingredients.

In the meantime, add the reserved marinade to the saucepan that is preheated over medium-high heat. Add the molasses, orange juice, and 1 tablespoon of soy sauce.

Bring to a simmer and then, whisk constantly until it gets syrupy. Brush the surface of duck breasts with glaze so they are completely covered.

Place duck breasts back in the Air Fryer basket; cook an additional 5 minutes. Enjoy!

Chinese-Style Sticky Turkey Thighs

Per serving:

279 Calories; 10.1g Fat; 19g Carbs; 27.7g Protein; 17.9g Sugars

Ingredients

1 tablespoon sesame oil 2 pounds turkey thighs

1 teaspoon Chinese Five-spice powder

1 teaspoon pink Himalayan salt 1/4 teaspoon Sichuan pepper

6 tablespoons honey

1 tablespoon Chinese rice vinegar 2 tablespoons soy sauce

1 tablespoon sweet chili sauce

1 tablespoon mustard

Directions

Preheat your Air Fryer to 360 degrees F.

Brush the sesame oil all over the turkey thighs. Season them with spices.

Cook for 23 minutes, turning over once or twice. Make sure to work in batches to ensure even cooking

In the meantime, combine the remaining ingredients in a wok (or similar type pan) that is preheated over medium-high heat. Cook and stir until the sauce reduces by about a third.

Add the fried turkey thighs to the wok; gently stir to coat with the sauce. Let the turkey rest for 10 minutes before slicing and serving. Enjoy!

Creole Turkey with Peppers

(Ready in about 35 minutes | Servings 4)

Per serving:

426 Calories; 15.4g Fat; 12.4g Carbs; 51g Protein; 6.1g Sugars

Ingredients

2 pounds turkey thighs, skinless and boneless 1 red onion, sliced

2 bell peppers, deveined and sliced

1 habanero pepper, deveined and minced 1 carrot, sliced

1 tablespoon Creole seasoning mix

1 tablespoon fish sauce 2 cups chicken broth

Directions

Preheat your Air Fryer to 360 degrees F. Now, spritz the bottom and sides of the casserole dish with a nonstick cooking spray.

Arrange the turkey thighs in the casserole dish. Add the onion, pepper, and carrot. Sprinkle with Creole seasoning.

Afterwards, add the fish sauce and chicken broth. Cook in the preheated Air Fryer for 30 minutes. Serve warm and enjoy!

Crunchy Munchy Chicken Tenders with Peanuts

(Ready in about 25 minutes | Servings 4)

Per serving

343 Calories; 16.4g Fat; 10.6g Carbs; 36.8g Protein; 1g Sugars

Ingredients

1 ½ pounds chicken tenderloins 2 tablespoons peanut oil

1/2 cup tortilla chips, crushed

Sea salt and ground black pepper, to taste 1/2 teaspoon garlic powder

1 teaspoon red pepper flakes

2 tablespoons peanuts, roasted and roughly chopped

Directions

Start by preheating your Air Fryer to 360 degrees F. Brush the chicken tenderloins with peanut oil on all sides.

In a mixing bowl, thoroughly combine the crushed chips, salt, black pepper,

garlic powder, and red pepper flakes. Dredge the chicken in the breading, shaking off any residual coating.

Lay the chicken tenderloins into the cooking basket. Cook for 12 to 13 minutes or until it is no longer pink in the center. Work in batches; an instant- read thermometer should read at least 165 degrees F.

 Serve garnished with roasted peanuts. Bon appétit!

Dijon Roasted Sausage and Carrots

(Ready in about 20 minutes | Servings 3)

Per serving:

313 Calories; 13.6g Fat; 14.7g Carbs; 32.3g Protein; 7.2g Sugars

Ingredients

1 pound chicken sausages, smoked

1 pound carrots, trimmed and halved lengthwise 1 tablespoon Dijon mustard

2 tablespoons olive oil 1/2 teaspoon sea salt

1/4 teaspoon ground black pepper

Directions

Start by preheating your Air Fryer to 380 degrees F. Pierce the sausages all over with a fork and add them to the cooking basket.

Add the carrots and the remaining ingredients; toss until well coated.

Cook for 10 minutes in the preheated Air Fryer. Shake the basket and cook an additional 5 to 7 minutes. Serve warm.

Easy Chicken Sliders

(Ready in about 30 minutes | Servings 3)

Per serving:

479 Calories; 17.9g Fat; 43g Carbs; 34.4g Protein; 1.3g Sugars

Ingredients

1/2 cup all-purpose flour 1 teaspoon garlic salt

1/2 teaspoon black pepper, preferably freshly ground

1 teaspoon celery seeds

1/2 teaspoon mustard seeds 1/2 teaspoon dried basil

1 egg

2 chicken breasts, cut in thirds 6 small-sized dinner rolls

Directions

In mixing bowl, thoroughly combine the flour and seasonings. In a separate shallow bowl, beat the egg until frothy.

Dredge the chicken through the flour mixture, then into egg; afterwards, roll them over the flour mixture again.

Spritz the chicken pieces with a cooking spray on all sides. Transfer them to the cooking basket.

Cook in the preheated Air Fryer at 380 degrees F for 15 minutes; turn them over and cook an additional 10 to 12 minutes.

Test for doneness and adjust the seasonings. Serve immediately on dinner rolls.

Easy Hot Chicken Drumsticks

(Ready in about 40 minutes | Servings 6)

Per serving:

280 Calories; 18.7g Fat; 2.6g Carbs; 24.1g Protein; 1.4g Sugars

Ingredients

6 chicken drumsticks Sauce:

6 ounces hot sauce

3 tablespoons olive oil

3 tablespoons tamari sauce 1 teaspoon dried thyme 1/2 teaspoon dried oregano

Directions

Spritz the sides and bottom of the cooking basket with a nonstick cooking spray.

Cook the chicken drumsticks at 380 degrees F for 35 minutes, flipping them over halfway through.

Meanwhile, heat the hot sauce, olive oil, tamari sauce, thyme, and oregano in a pan over medium-low heat; reserve.

Drizzle the sauce over the prepared chicken drumsticks; toss to coat well and serve. Bon appétit!

Easy Ritzy Chicken Nuggets

(Ready in about 20 minutes | Servings 4)

Per serving:

355 Calories; 20.1g Fat; 5.3g Carbs; 36.6g Protein; 0.2g Sugars

Ingredients

1 ½ pounds chicken tenderloins, cut into small pieces 1/2 teaspoon garlic salt

1/2 teaspoon cayenne pepper

1/4 teaspoon black pepper, freshly cracked 4 tablespoons olive oil

1/3 cup saltines (e.g. Ritz crackers), crushed

4 tablespoons Parmesan cheese, freshly grated

Directions

Start by preheating your Air Fryer to 390 degrees F.

Season each piece of the chicken with garlic salt, cayenne pepper, and black pepper.

In a mixing bowl, thoroughly combine the olive oil with crushed saltines. Dip each piece of chicken in the cracker mixture.

Finally, roll the chicken pieces over the Parmesan cheese. Cook for 8 minutes, working in batches.

Later, if you want to warm the chicken nuggets, add them to the basket and cook for 1 minute more. Serve with French fries, if desired.

Farmhouse Roast Turkey

(Ready in about 50 minutes | Servings 6)

Per serving:

316 Calories; 24.2g Fat; 2.5g Carbs; 20.4g Protein; 1.1g Sugars

Ingredients

2 pounds turkey

1 tablespoon fresh rosemary, chopped 1 teaspoon sea salt

1/2 teaspoon ground black pepper 1 onion, chopped

1 celery stalk, chopped

Directions

Start by preheating your Air Fryer to 360 degrees F. Spritz the sides and bottom of the cooking basket with a nonstick cooking spray.

Place the turkey in the cooking basket. Add the rosemary, salt, and black pepper. Cook for 30 minutes in the preheated Air Fryer.

Add the onion and celery and cook an additional 15 minutes. Bon appétit!

Garden Vegetable and Chicken Casserole

(Ready in about 30 minutes | Servings 4)

Per serving:

333 Calories; 10.7g Fat; 5.4g Carbs; 50g Protein; 1.2g Sugars

Ingredients

2 teaspoons peanut oil

2 pounds chicken drumettes 1 garlic clove, minced

1/2 medium-sized leek, sliced 2 carrots, sliced

1 cup cauliflower florets

1 tablespoon all-purpose flour 2 cups vegetable broth

1/4 cup dry white wine

1 thyme sprig

1 rosemary sprig

Directions

Preheat your Air Fryer to 370 degrees F. Then, drizzle the chicken drumettes with peanut oil and cook them for 10 minutes. Transfer the chicken drumettes to a lightly greased pan.

Add the garlic, leeks, carrots, and cauliflower.

Mix the remaining ingredients in a bowl. Pour the flour mixture into the pan. Cook at 380 degrees F for 15 minutes.

Serve warm.

Italian Chicken and Cheese Frittata

(Ready in about 25 minutes | Servings 4)

Per serving:

329 Calories; 25.3g Fat; 3.4g Carbs; 21.1g Protein; 2.3g Sugars

Ingredients

1 (1-pound) fillet chicken breast

Sea salt and ground black pepper, to taste 1 tablespoon olive oil

4 eggs

1/2 teaspoon cayenne pepper 1/2 cup Mascarpone cream

1/4 cup Asiago cheese, freshly grated

Directions

Flatten the chicken breast with a meat mallet. Season with salt and pepper.

Heat the olive oil in a frying pan over medium flame. Cook the chicken for 10 to 12 minutes; slice into small strips, and reserve.

Then, in a mixing bowl, thoroughly combine the eggs, and cayenne pepper; season with salt to taste. Add the cheese and stir to combine.

Add the reserved chicken. Then, pour the mixture into a lightly greased pan; put the pan into the cooking basket.

Cook in the preheated Air Fryer at 355 degrees F for 10 minutes, flipping over halfway through.

Lemon-Basil Turkey Breast

(Ready in about 1 hour | Servings 4)

Per serving:

416 Calories; 22.6g Fat; 0g Carbs; 49g Protein; 0g Sugars

Ingredients

2 tablespoons olive oil

2 pounds turkey breasts, bone-in skin-on

Coarse sea salt and ground black pepper, to taste 1 teaspoon fresh basil leaves, chopped

2 tablespoons lemon zest, grated

Directions

Rub olive oil on all sides of the turkey breasts; sprinkle with salt, pepper, basil, and lemon zest.

Place the turkey breasts skin side up on a parchment-lined cooking basket.

Cook in the preheated Air Fryer at 330 degrees F for 30 minutes. Now, turn them over and cook an additional 28 minutes.

Serve with lemon wedges, if desired. Bon appétit!

Loaded Chicken Burgers

(Ready in about 30 minutes | Servings 5)

Per serving:

476 Calories; 25.9g Fat; 29.9g Carbs; 31.7g Protein; 2.5g Sugars

Ingredients

2 tablespoons olive oil 1 onion, finely chopped 2 green garlic, chopped

6 ounces mushrooms, chopped 1 ½ pounds ground chicken 1/3 cup parmesan cheese

1/4 cup pork rinds, crushed 1 tablespoon fish sauce

1 tablespoon tamari sauce

1 teaspoon Dijon mustard 5 soft hamburger buns

5 lettuce leaves

Directions

Heat a nonstick skillet over medium-high heat; add olive oil. Once hot, sauté the onion until tender and translucent, about 3 minutes.

Add the garlic and mushrooms and cook an additional 2 minutes, stirring frequently.

Add the ground chicken, cheese, pork rind, fish sauce, and tamari sauce; mix until everything is well incorporated.

Form the mixture into 5 patties. Transfer the patties to the lightly greased cooking basket.

Cook in the preheated Air Fryer at 370 degrees F for 8 minutes; then, flip them over and cook for 8 minutes on the other side.

Serve on burger buns, garnished with mustard and lettuce. Bon appétit!

Marinated Chicken Drumettes with Asparagus

(Ready in about 30 minutes + marinating time | Servings 6)

Per serving:

356 Calories; 22.1g Fat; 7.8g Carbs; 31.4g Protein; 4.1g Sugars

Ingredients

6 chicken drumettes

1 ½ pounds asparagus, ends trimmed Marinade:

3 tablespoons canola oil 3 tablespoons soy sauce 3 tablespoons lime juice

3 heaping tablespoons shallots, minced 1 heaping teaspoon fresh garlic, minced

1 (1-inch) piece fresh ginger, peeled and minced

1 teaspoon Creole seasoning

Coarse sea salt and ground black pepper, to taste

Directions

In a ceramic bowl, mix all ingredients for the marinade. Add the chicken drumettes and let them marinate at least 5 hours in the refrigerator.

Now, drain the chicken drumettes and discard the marinade.

Cook in the preheated Air Fryer at 370 degrees F for 11 minutes. Turn the chicken drumettes over and cook for a further 11 minutes.

While the chicken drumettes are cooking, add the reserved marinade to the preheated skillet. Add the asparagus and cook for approximately 5 minutes or until cooked through. Serve with the air-fried chicken and enjoy!

Mediterranean Chicken Breasts with Roasted Tomatoes

(Ready in about 1 hour | Servings 8)

Per serving:

315 Calories; 17.1g Fat; 2.7g Carbs; 36g Protein; 1.7g Sugars

Ingredients

2 teaspoons olive oil, melted

3 pounds chicken breasts, bone-in

1/2 teaspoon black pepper, freshly ground 1/2 teaspoon salt

1 teaspoon cayenne pepper

2 tablespoons fresh parsley, minced 1 teaspoon fresh basil, minced

1 teaspoon fresh rosemary, minced

4 medium-sized Roma tomatoes, halved

Directions

Start by preheating your Air Fryer to 370 degrees F. Brush the cooking basket with 1 teaspoon of olive oil.

Sprinkle the chicken breasts with all seasonings listed above.

Cook for 25 minutes or until chicken breasts are slightly browned. Work in batches.

Arrange the tomatoes in the cooking basket and brush them with the

remaining teaspoon of olive oil. Season with sea salt.

Cook the tomatoes at 350 degrees F for 10 minutes, shaking halfway through the cooking time. Serve with chicken breasts. Bon appétit!

Old-Fashioned Chicken Drumettes

(Ready in about 30 minutes | Servings 3)

Per serving:

347 Calories; 9.1g Fat; 11.3g Carbs; 41g Protein; 0.1g Sugars

Ingredients

1/3 cup all-purpose flour

1/2 teaspoon ground white pepper 1 teaspoon seasoning salt

1 teaspoon garlic paste 1 teaspoon rosemary

1 whole egg + 1 egg white

6 chicken drumettes

1 heaping tablespoon fresh chives, chopped

Directions

Start by preheating your Air Fryer to 390 degrees.

Mix the flour with white pepper, salt, garlic paste, and rosemary in a small-sized bowl.

In another bowl, beat the eggs until frothy.

Dip the chicken into the flour mixture, then into the beaten eggs; coat with the flour mixture one more time.

Cook the chicken drumettes for 22 minutes. Serve warm, garnished with chives.

Paprika Chicken Legs with Brussels Sprouts

(Ready in about 30 minutes | Servings 2)

Per serving:

355 Calories; 20.1g Fat; 5.3g Carbs; 36.6g Protein; 0.2g Sugars

Ingredients

2 chicken legs

1/2 teaspoon paprika 1/2 teaspoon kosher salt

1/2 teaspoon black pepper 1 pound Brussels sprouts

1 teaspoon dill, fresh or dried

Directions

Start by preheating your Air Fryer to 370 degrees F.

Now, season your chicken with paprika, salt, and pepper. Transfer the chicken legs to the cooking basket. Cook for 10 minutes.

Flip the chicken legs and cook an additional 10 minutes. Reserve.

Add the Brussels sprouts to the cooking basket; sprinkle with dill. Cook at 380 degrees F for 15 minutes, shaking the basket halfway through.

Serve with the reserved chicken legs. Bon appétit!

Peanut Chicken and Pepper Wraps

(Ready in about 25 minutes | Servings 4)

Per serving:

529 Calories; 25.5g Fat; 31.5g Carbs; 40.1g Protein; 6.8g Sugars

Pretzel Crusted Chicken with Spicy Mustard Sauce

(Ready in about 20 minutes | Servings 6)

Per serving:

357 Calories; 17.6g Fat; 20.3g Carbs; 28.1g Protein; 2.8g Sugars

Ingredients

2 eggs

1 ½ pound chicken breasts, boneless, skinless, cut into bite-sized chunks
1/2 cup crushed pretzels

1 teaspoon shallot powder 1 teaspoon paprika

Sea salt and ground black pepper, to taste

1/2 cup vegetable broth 1 tablespoon cornstarch

3 tablespoons Worcestershire sauce

3 tablespoons tomato paste

1 tablespoon apple cider vinegar 2 tablespoons olive oil

2 garlic cloves, chopped

1 jalapeno pepper, minced 1 teaspoon yellow mustard

Directions

Start by preheating your Air Fryer to 390 degrees F.

In a mixing dish, whisk the eggs until frothy; toss the chicken chunks into the whisked eggs and coat well.

In another dish, combine the crushed pretzels with shallot powder, paprika, salt and pepper. Then, lay the chicken chunks in the pretzel mixture; turn it over until well coated.

Place the chicken pieces in the air fryer basket. Cook the chicken for 12 minutes, shaking the basket halfway through.

Meanwhile, whisk the vegetable broth with cornstarch, Worcestershire sauce, tomato paste, and apple cider vinegar.

Preheat a cast-iron skillet over medium flame. Heat the olive oil and sauté the garlic with jalapeno pepper for 30 to 40 seconds, stirring frequently.

Add the cornstarch mixture and let it simmer until the sauce has thickened a little. Now, add the air-fried chicken and mustard; let it simmer for 2 minutes more or until heated through.

Serve immediately and enjoy!

Quick and Easy Chicken Mole

(Ready in about 35 minutes | Servings 4)

Per serving:

453 Calories; 17.5g Fat; 25.1g Carbs; 47.5g Protein; 12.9g Sugars

Ingredients

8 chicken thighs, skinless, bone-in 1 tablespoon peanut oil

Sea salt and ground black pepper, to taste

Mole sauce:

1 tablespoon peanut oil 1 onion, chopped

1 ounce dried negro chiles, stemmed, seeded, and chopped 2 garlic cloves, peeled and halved

2 large-sized fresh tomatoes, pureed

2 tablespoons raisins

1 ½ ounces bittersweet chocolate, chopped 1 teaspoon dried Mexican oregano

1/2 teaspoon ground cumin 1 teaspoon coriander seeds A pinch of ground cloves 4 strips orange peel

1/4 cup almonds, sliced and toasted

Directions

Start by preheating your Air Fryer to 380 degrees F. Toss the chicken thighs with the peanut oil, salt, and black pepper.

Cook in the preheated Air Fryer for 12 minutes; flip them and cook an additional 10 minutes; reserve.

To make the sauce, heat 1 tablespoon of peanut oil in a saucepan over medium-high heat. Now, sauté the onion, chiles and garlic until fragrant or about 2 minutes.

Next, stir in the tomatoes, raisins, chocolate, oregano, cumin, coriander seeds, and cloves. Let it simmer until the sauce has slightly thickened.

Add the reserved chicken to the baking pan; add the sauce and cook in the preheated Air Fryer at 360 degrees F for 10 minutes or until thoroughly warmed.

Serve garnished with orange peel and sliced almonds. Enjoy!

Ranch Parmesan Chicken Wings

(Ready in about 25 minutes | Servings 3)

Per serving:

521 Calories; 34.2g Fat; 17.3g Carbs; 33.7g Protein; 1.4g Sugars

Ingredients

1/2 cup seasoned breadcrumbs 2 tablespoons butter, melted

6 tablespoons parmesan cheese, preferably freshly grated

1 tablespoon Ranch seasoning mix 2 tablespoons oyster sauce

6 chicken wings, bone-in

Directions

Start by preheating your Air Fryer to 370 degrees F.

In a resealable bag, place the breadcrumbs, butter, parmesan, Ranch seasoning mix, and oyster sauce. Add the chicken wings and shake to coat on all sides.

Arrange the chicken wings in the Air Fryer basket. Spritz the chicken wings with a nonstick cooking spray.

Cook for 11 minutes. Turn them over and cook an additional 11 minutes. Serve warm with your favorite dipping sauce, if desired. Enjoy!

Roasted Citrus Turkey Drumsticks

(Ready in about 55 minutes | Servings 3)

Per serving:

352 Calories; 23.4g Fat; 5.2g Carbs; 29.3g Protein; 2.6g Sugars

Ingredients

3 medium turkey drumsticks, bone-in skin-on 1/2 butter stick, melted

Sea salt and ground black pepper, to taste

1 teaspoon cayenne pepper

1 teaspoon fresh garlic, minced 1 teaspoon dried parsley flakes 1 teaspoon onion powder

Zest of one orange 1/4 cup orange juice

Directions

Rub all ingredients onto the turkey drumsticks.

Preheat your Air Fryer to 400 degrees F. Cook the turkey drumsticks for 16 minutes in the preheated Air Fryer.

Loosely cover with foil and cook an additional 24 minutes.

Once cooked, let it rest for 10 minutes before slicing and serving. Bon appétit!

Rustic Chicken Legs with Turnip Chips

(Ready in about 30 minutes | Servings 3)

Per serving:

207 Calories; 7.8g Fat; 3.4g Carbs; 29.5g Protein; 1.6g Sugars

Ingredients

1 pound chicken legs

1 teaspoon Himalayan salt 1 teaspoon paprika

1/2 teaspoon ground black pepper

1 teaspoon butter, melted

1 turnip, trimmed and sliced

Directions

Spritz the sides and bottom of the cooking basket with a nonstick cooking spray.

Season the chicken legs with salt, paprika, and ground black pepper.

Cook at 370 degrees F for 10 minutes. Increase the temperature to 380 degrees F.

Drizzle turnip slices with melted butter and transfer them to the cooking basket with the chicken. Cook the turnips and chicken for 15 minutes more, flipping them halfway through the cooking time.

As for the chicken, an instant-read thermometer should read at least 165 degrees F.

Serve and enjoy!

Sausage, Ham and Hash Brown Bake

(Ready in about 45 minutes | Servings 4)

Per serving:

509 Calories; 20.1g Fat; 40g Carbs; 41.2g Protein; 3.9g Sugars

Ingredients

1/2 pound chicken sausages, smoked 1/2 pound ham, sliced

6 ounces hash browns, frozen and shredded

2 garlic cloves, minced 8 ounces spinach

1/2 cup Ricotta cheese

1/2 cup Asiago cheese, grated 4 eggs

1/2 cup yogurt

1/2 cup milk

Salt and ground black pepper, to taste 1 teaspoon smoked paprika

81

Directions

Start by preheating your Air Fryer to 380 degrees F. Cook the sausages and ham for 10 minutes; set aside.

Meanwhile, in a preheated saucepan, cook the hash browns and garlic for 4 minutes, stirring frequently; remove from the heat, add the spinach and cover with the lid.

Allow the spinach to wilt completely. Transfer the sautéed mixture to a baking pan. Add the reserved sausage and ham.

In a mixing dish, thoroughly combine the cheese, eggs, yogurt, milk, salt, pepper, and paprika. Pour the cheese mixture over the hash browns in the pan.

Place the baking pan in the cooking basket and cook approximately 30 minutes or until everything is thoroughly cooked. Bon appétit!

Smoked Duck with Rosemary-Infused Gravy

(Ready in about 30 minutes | Servings 4)

Per serving:

485 Calories; 19.7g Fat; 24.1g Carbs; 51.3g Protein; 15.6g Sugars

Ingredients

1 ½ pounds smoked duck breasts, boneless 1 tablespoon yellow mustard

2 tablespoons ketchup

1 teaspoon agave syrup 12 pearl onions peeled 1 tablespoon flour

5 ounces chicken broth

1 teaspoon rosemary, finely chopped

Directions

Cook the smoked duck breasts in the preheated Air Fryer at 365 degrees F for 15 minutes.

Smear the mustard, ketchup, and agave syrup on the duck breast. Top with pearl onions. Cook for a further 7 minutes or until the skin of the duck breast looks crispy and golden brown.

Slice the duck breasts and reserve. Drain off the duck fat from the pan.

 Then, add the reserved 1 tablespoon of duck fat to the pan and warm it over medium heat; add flour and cook until your roux is dark brown.

Add the chicken broth and rosemary to the pan. Reduce the heat to low and cook until the gravy has thickened slightly. Spoon the warm gravy over the reserved duck breasts. Enjoy!

Spice Lime Chicken Tenders

(Ready in about 20 minutes | Servings 6)

Per serving:

422 Calories; 29.2g Fat; 6.1g Carbs; 32.9g Protein; 2.4g Sugars

Ingredients

1 lime

2 pounds chicken tenderloins cut up 1 cup cornflakes, crushed

1/2 cup Parmesan cheese, grated 1 tablespoon olive oil

Sea salt and ground black pepper, to taste

1 teaspoon cayenne pepper 1/3 teaspoon ground cumin 1 teaspoon chili powder

1 egg

Directions

Squeeze the lime juice all over the chicken.

Spritz the cooking basket with a nonstick cooking spray.

In a mixing bowl, thoroughly combine the cornflakes, Parmesan, olive oil, salt, black pepper, cayenne pepper, cumin, and chili powder.

In another shallow bowl, whisk the egg until well beaten. Dip the chicken tenders in the egg, then in cornflakes mixture.

Transfer the breaded chicken to the prepared cooking basket. Cook in the preheated Air Fryer at 380 degrees F for 12 minutes. Turn them over halfway through the cooking time. Work in batches. Serve immediately.

Summer Meatballs with Cheese

(Ready in about 15 minutes | Servings 4)

Per serving:

497 Calories; 24g Fat; 20.7g Carbs; 41.9g Protein; 4.1g Sugars

Ingredients

1 pound ground turkey 1/2 pound ground pork 1 egg, well beaten

1 cup seasoned breadcrumbs 1 teaspoon dried basil

1 teaspoon dried rosemary

1/4 cup Manchego cheese, grated

2 tablespoons yellow onions, finely chopped 1 teaspoon fresh garlic, finely chopped

Sea salt and ground black pepper, to taste

Directions

In a mixing bowl, combine all the ingredients until everything is well incorporated.

Shape the mixture into 1-inch balls.

Cook the meatballs in the preheated Air Fryer at 380 degrees for 7 minutes. Shake halfway through the cooking time. Work in batches.

Serve with your favorite pasta. Bon appétit!

Tarragon Turkey Tenderloins with Baby Potatoes

(Ready in about 50 minutes | Servings 6)

Per serving:

317 Calories; 7.4g Fat; 14.2g Carbs; 45.7g Protein; 1.1g Sugars

Ingredients

2 pounds turkey tenderloins 2 teaspoons olive oil

Salt and ground black pepper, to taste

1 teaspoon smoked paprika

2 tablespoons dry white wine

1 tablespoon fresh tarragon leaves, chopped 1 pound baby potatoes, rubbed

Directions

Brush the turkey tenderloins with olive oil. Season with salt, black pepper, and paprika.

Afterwards, add the white wine and tarragon.

Cook the turkey tenderloins at 350 degrees F for 30 minutes, flipping them over halfway through. Let them rest for 5 to 9 minutes before slicing and serving.

After that, spritz the sides and bottom of the cooking basket with the remaining 1 teaspoon of olive oil.

Then, preheat your Air Fryer to 400 degrees F; cook the baby potatoes for 15 minutes. Serve with the turkey and enjoy!

Thai Red Duck with Candy Onion

(Ready in about 25 minutes | Servings 4)

Per serving:

362 Calories; 18.7g Fat; 4g Carbs; 42.3g Protein; 1.3g Sugars

Ingredients

1 ½ pounds duck breasts, skin removed 1 teaspoon kosher salt

1/2 teaspoon cayenne pepper

1/3 teaspoon black pepper 1/2 teaspoon smoked paprika

1 tablespoon Thai red curry paste

1 cup candy onions, halved

1/4 small pack coriander, chopped

Directions

Place the duck breasts between 2 sheets of foil; then, use a rolling pin to bash the duck until they are 1-inch thick.

Preheat your Air Fryer to 395 degrees F.

Rub the duck breasts with salt, cayenne pepper, black pepper, paprika, and red curry paste. Place the duck breast in the cooking basket.

Cook for 11 to 12 minutes. Top with candy onions and cook for another 10 to 11 minutes.

Serve garnished with coriander and enjoy!

Thanksgiving Turkey Tenderloin with Gravy

(Ready in about 40 minutes | Servings 4)

Per serving:

374 Calories; 8.1g Fat; 20.5g Carbs; 52g Protein; 10.2g Sugars

Ingredients

2 ½ pounds turkey tenderloin, sliced into pieces 1/2 head of garlic, peeled and halved

1 dried marjoram

Sea salt and ground black pepper, to taste 1 teaspoon cayenne pepper

Gravy:

3 cups vegetable broth 1/3 cup all-purpose flour

Sea salt and ground black pepper, to taste

Directions

Start by preheating your Air Fryer to 350 degrees F.

Rub the turkey tenderloins with garlic halves; add marjoram, salt, black pepper, and cayenne pepper.

Cook the turkey tenderloins at 350 degrees F for 30 minutes or until an instant-read thermometer inserted into the center of the breast reaches 165 degrees F; flip them over halfway through.

In a saucepan, place the drippings from the roasted turkey. Add 1 cup of broth and 1/6 cup of flour to the pan; whisk until it makes a smooth paste.

Once it gets a golden brown color, add the rest of the chicken broth and flour. Sprinkle with salt and pepper to taste.

Let it simmer over medium heat, stirring constantly for 6 to 7 minutes. Serve with warm turkey tenderloin and enjoy!

The Best Chicken Burgers Ever

(Ready in about 20 minutes | Servings 4)

Per serving:

507 Calories; 26.5g Fat; 37.6g Carbs; 30g Protein; 12.8g Sugars

Ingredients

1 tablespoon olive oil

1 onion, peeled and finely chopped 2 garlic cloves, minced

Sea salt and ground black pepper, to taste 1/2 teaspoon paprika

1/2 teaspoon ground cumin

1 pound chicken breast, ground 4 soft rolls

4 tablespoons ketchup

4 tablespoons mayonnaise 2 teaspoons Dijon mustard

4 tablespoons green onions, chopped

4 pickles, sliced

Directions

Heat the olive oil in a skillet over high flame. Then, sauté the onion until golden and translucent, about 4 minutes.

Add the garlic and cook an additional 30 seconds or until it is aromatic.

Season with salt, pepper, paprika, and cumin; reserve.

Add the chicken and cook for 2 to 3 minutes, stirring and crumbling with a fork. Add the onion mixture and mix to combine well.

Shape the mixture into patties and transfer them to the cooking basket. Cook in the preheated Air Fryer at 360 degrees F for 6 minutes. Turn them over and cook an additional 5 minutes. Work in batches.

Smear the base of the roll with ketchup, mayo, and mustard. Top with the chicken, green onions, and pickles. Enjoy!

Traditional Chicken Teriyaki

(Ready in about 50 minutes | Servings 4)

Per serving:

362 Calories; 21.1g Fat; 4.4g Carbs; 36.6g Protein; 2.4g Sugars

Ingredients

1 ½ pounds chicken breast, halved 1 tablespoon lemon juice

2 tablespoons Mirin

1/4 cup milk

2 tablespoons soy sauce 1 tablespoon olive oil

1 teaspoon ginger, peeled and grated 2 garlic cloves, minced

1/2 teaspoon salt

1/2 teaspoon ground black pepper 1 teaspoon cornstarch

Directions

In a large ceramic dish, place the chicken, lemon juice, Mirin, milk, soy sauce, olive oil, ginger, and garlic. Let it marinate for 30 minutes in your refrigerator.

Spritz the sides and bottom of the cooking basket with a nonstick cooking spray. Arrange the chicken in the cooking basket and cook at 370 degrees F for 10 minutes.

Turn over the chicken, baste with the reserved marinade and cook for 4 minutes longer. Taste for doneness, season with salt and pepper, and reserve.

Mix the cornstarch with 1 tablespoon of water. Add the marinade to the preheated skillet over medium heat; cook for 3 to 4 minutes. Now, stir in the cornstarch slurry and cook until the sauce thickens.

Spoon the sauce over the reserved chicken and serve immediately.

Turkey and Sausage Meatloaf with Herbs

(Ready in about 45 minutes | Servings 4)

Per serving:

431 Calories; 22.3g Fat; 32.6g Carbs; 25.9g Protein; 18.5g Sugars

Ingredients

1/2 cup milk

4 bread slices, crustless 1 tablespoon olive oil

1 onion, finely chopped 1 garlic clove, minced 1/2 pound ground turkey

1/2 pound ground breakfast sausage 1 duck egg, whisked

1 teaspoon rosemary

1 teaspoon basil

1 teaspoon thyme

1 teaspoon cayenne pepper

Kosher salt and ground black pepper, to taste 1/2 cup ketchup

2 tablespoons molasses

1 tablespoon brown mustard

Directions

In a shallow bowl, pour the milk over the bread and let it soak in for 5 to 6 minutes.

Heat 1 tablespoon of oil over medium-high heat in a nonstick pan. Sauté the onions and garlic until tender and fragrant, about 2 minutes.

Add the turkey, sausage, egg, rosemary, basil, thyme, cayenne pepper, salt, and ground black pepper. Stir in the milk-soaked bread. Mix until everything is well incorporated.

Shape the mixture into a loaf and transfer it to a pan that is lightly greased with an olive oil mister.

Next, lower the pan onto the cooking basket.

In a mixing bowl, whisk the ketchup with molasses and mustard. Spread this mixture over the top of your meatloaf.

Cook approximately 27 minutes or until the meatloaf is no longer pink in the middle. Allow it to sit 10 minutes before slicing and serving. Bon appétit!

Turkey Bacon with Scrambled Eggs

(Ready in about 25 minutes | Servings 4)

Per serving:

456 Calories; 38.3g Fat; 6.3g Carbs; 21.4g Protein; 4.5g Sugars

Ingredients

1/2 pound turkey bacon 4 eggs

1/3 cup milk

2 tablespoons yogurt 1/2 teaspoon sea salt

1 bell pepper, finely chopped

2 green onions, finely chopped 1/2 cup Colby cheese, shredded

Directions

Place the turkey bacon in the cooking basket.

Cook at 360 degrees F for 9 to 11 minutes. Work in batches. Reserve the fried bacon.

In a mixing bowl, thoroughly whisk the eggs with milk and yogurt. Add salt, bell pepper, and green onions.

Brush the sides and bottom of the baking pan with the reserved 1 teaspoon of bacon grease.

Pour the egg mixture into the baking pan. Cook at 355 degrees F about 5 minutes. Top with shredded Colby cheese and cook for 5 to 6 minutes more.

Serve the scrambled eggs with the reserved bacon and enjoy!

Turkey Wings with Butter Roasted Potatoes

(Ready in about 55 minutes | Servings 4)

Per serving:

567 Calories; 14.3g Fat; 65.7g Carbs; 46.1g Protein; 2.9g Sugars

Ingredients

4 large-sized potatoes, peeled and cut into 1-inch chunks 1 tablespoon butter, melted

1 teaspoon rosemary

1 teaspoon garlic salt

1/2 teaspoon ground black pepper 1 ½ pounds turkey wings

2 tablespoons olive oil 2 garlic cloves, minced

1 tablespoon Dijon mustard

1/2 teaspoon cayenne pepper

Directions

Add the potatoes, butter, rosemary, salt, and pepper to the cooking basket.

Cook at 400 degrees F for 12 minutes. Reserve the potatoes, keeping them warm.

Now, place the turkey wings in the cooking basket that is previously cleaned

and greased with olive oil. Add the garlic, mustard, and cayenne pepper.

Cook in the preheated Air Fryer at 350 degrees f for 25 minutes. Turn them over and cook an additional 15 minutes.

Test for doneness with a meat thermometer. Serve with warm potatoes.

Alphabetic Index

CPSIA information can be obtained
at www.ICGtesting.com
Printed in the USA
BVHW090938270521
608293BV00003B/700